Pint-Sized Puppets and Poems

by
Cara Bradshaw

illustrated by
Cara Bradshaw

Cover by Teresa Mathis

ISBN No. 0-86653-785-6

Printing No. 987654321

Good Apple
1204 Buchanan St., Box 299
Carthage, IL 62321-0299

Paramount Publishing

Introduction

Puppets provide an excellent educational opportunity for children of all ages. For younger children, puppets are effective teaching tools that provide entertainment while developing motor skills. Puppets help older children to stimulate original thinking, imagination, and creative expression in presenting their own puppet shows. Create your own lovable puppets out of Pellon™ fabric or make paper stick puppets.

Contents

Supplies

Pellon™ Puppets

heavy weight Pellon™ (or felt)
permanent felt-tip marker (fine tip)
color mediums

- crayons
- fabric paints
- plastic markers
- pastels
- needle and thread

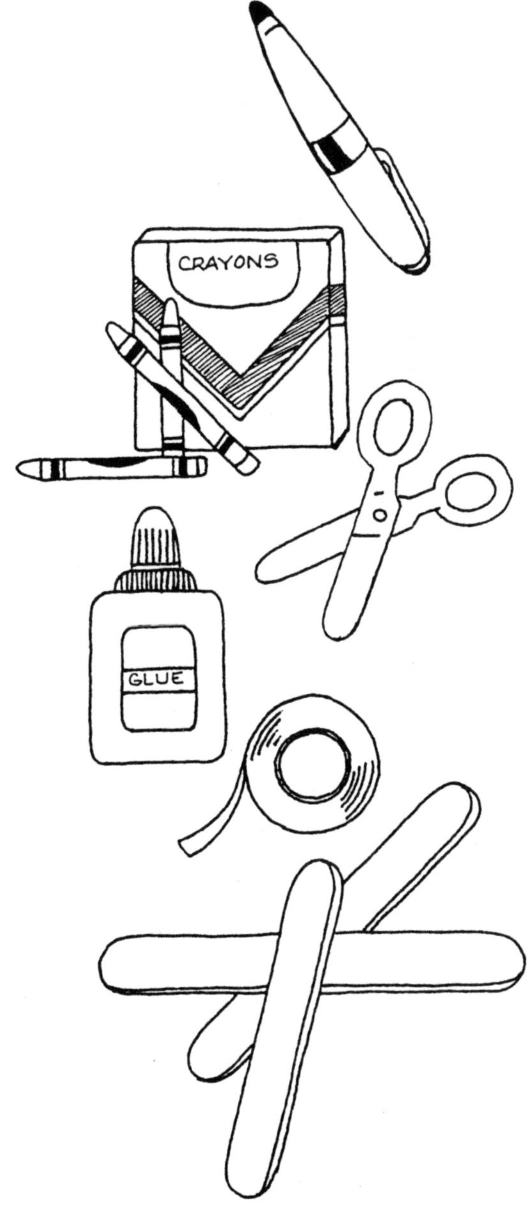

Stick Puppets

types of paper that can be used

- cardstock
- poster board
- construction paper
- typing paper
- tracing paper

color mediums

- crayons
- markers
- plastic markers
- colored pencils

lamination or clear Con-Tact™ paper

craft sticks

Instructions

Pellon™ Puppets

1. Lay Pellon™ over pattern. Trace with permanent felt-tip pen (fine tip).
2. Cut out along dotted lines.
3. Color picture with chosen color medium. See color-shading tip.*
4. Lay finished picture faceup on another piece of Pellon™ or felt and sew around the outside line of the picture leaving a hole between Xs. Backstitch by each X. This will provide a space for the finger.
5. Cut out the bottom layer of Pellon™ or felt to match the top piece. The puppet is ready for finger play.

*Color-Shading Tip (Optional)

Add some fun to your puppets with a touch of shading. This can be done with most color mediums. (An example of a pumpkin has been demonstrated.) Color the pumpkin orange. Around curves where the illustration is shaded lightly, color darker with orange. With a little touch of black, outline around darker shaded areas as seen on the illustration. The mouth is done with yellow, shaded with orange and a touch of black to enhance shadowing. If the puppet is white, shade with a little grey or a light touch of black to add a little dimension.

Paper Stick Puppets

1. Photocopy a pattern of the puppet onto cardstock or other paper. (If using typing or tracing paper, trace the pattern and then mount on poster board or construction paper for added strength.)
2. Color with your chosen color medium. (See color-shading tip on page 2.)
3. Cut out along the border to provide a margin for the puppets. (A dotted outline is provided for fabric puppets. Paper puppets do not need as wide a border.)
4. Laminate or cover both sides with clear Con-Tact™ paper.

   Note: To keep from peeling, trim along the outside leaving a narrow border (about an $^1/_8$" [0.3 cm] margin) from paper puppet.
5. Glue or tape a craft stick to the back.

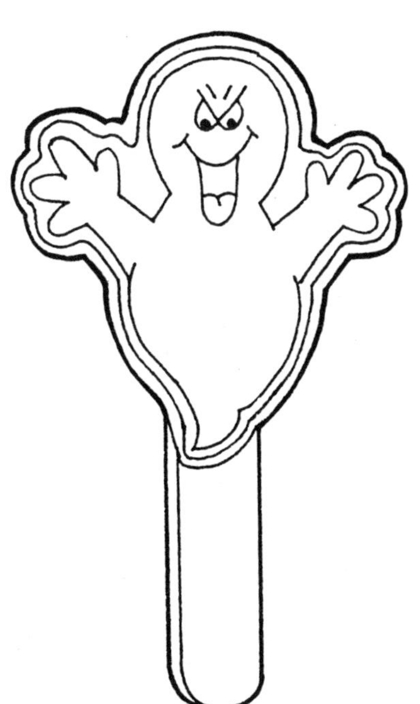

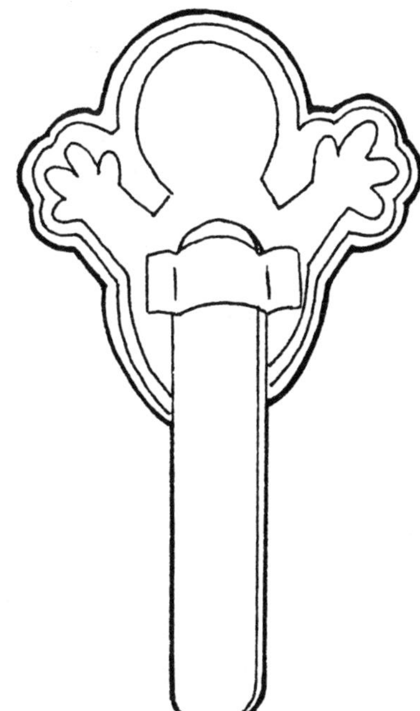

Ideas

Finger-play puppets are designed to be used with traditional favorite stories, songs, and poems. Included in the following pages are selected finger plays and poems to be used along with other favorites that have become popular over the years. Not all of the illustrations have verses, so feel free to explore your imagination.

These illustrations can also be used in many fun and creative ways.

Suggestions:

- bookmarks
- calendar cutouts
- scrapbook decorations
- counting and color definition
- all-occasion cards children can color themselves
- flash cards
- flannel board stories
- visual aids
- reward badges

Examples

Use the circle and square below to make reward badges.

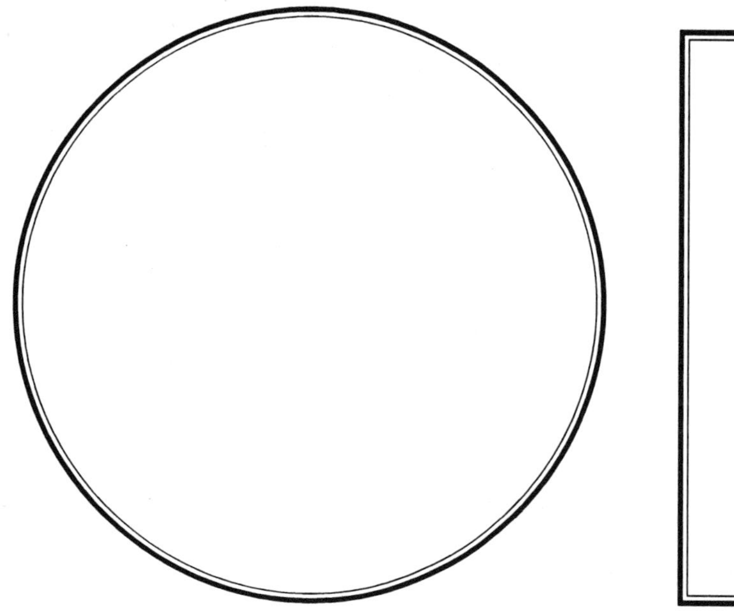

Ideas

The "family" puppets (on pages 9 and 10) can be useful in helping a child cope with problems that arise in his or her young life. The "bear family" puppets can also be effective for a child to learn how a certain bear character deals with problems.

Dramatize the problem, letting the child be the lead player. Give the child suggestions on how to act, and let him or her role-play the problem to reach a solution. Here are a few ideas.

How to deal with:

- a new baby in the house
- the first day at school
- a word about strangers
- a visit with Grandma and Grandpa
- Dad having to work late
- Dad or Mom leaving for awhile (separation or divorce)
- self-esteem (how I feel about myself)
- a visit to the doctor or dentist
- stealing
- lying
- teasing
- manners
- fighting
- my friends not liking me
- keeping my body healthy
- safety in the world around me

Use the bear pattern on page 20 for the bear family. Trace the accessories onto the paper first; then trace the bears. Examples of finished bears are illustrated below.

Bear Accessories

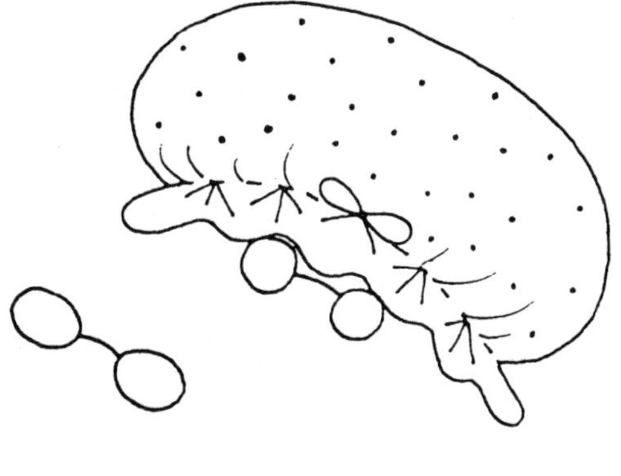

Create a Puppet Show

Use finger-play puppets in a puppet show by constructing a stage. Examples of different varieties are shown below.

Example 1

Example 1:

Use a cardboard box, shoe box, or larger box with the middle and bottom or top of the box cut out. Let the children color backgrounds of different scenes where the action can take place (outside, in a house, etc.).

Example 2:

Hang a sheet, tablecloth, or piece of fabric from a doorway. Make a casing by basting a seam or using safety pins.

Methods of Hanging:

a. Insert a string or rope through the casing and tack the ends to a doorway.
b. Use a spring-action curtain rod.

Example 2

cut along dotted lines

Example 3:

Use a table or packing box draped with a cloth.

Example 4:

Make a portable stage by using a three-panel screen. Make the frame out of wood, using metal angles in the corners of the frame for added strength. Cover the wood frame with canvas, an old sheet (hem or zigzag around the edges), or cardboard panels, and fasten onto the frame with tacks or a staple gun. Use double-action hinges on the top and bottom of the center panel and attach to the side panels.

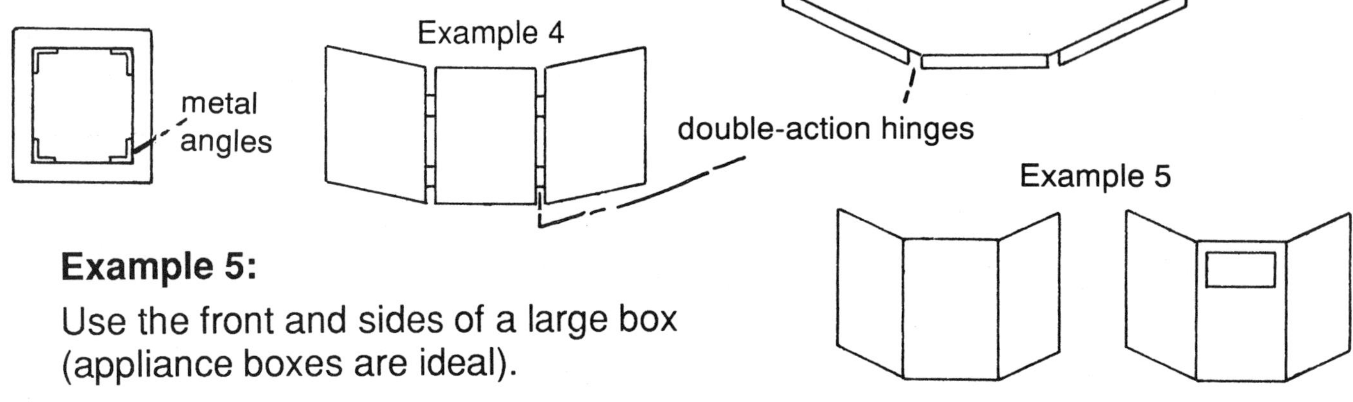

Example 5:

Use the front and sides of a large box (appliance boxes are ideal).

Puppet Patterns

It could be a ghost or a low-flying bat, . . .
Too bad I'm not an elephant,
My nose would be quite long, . . .
The sun is here to warm your wings, . . .

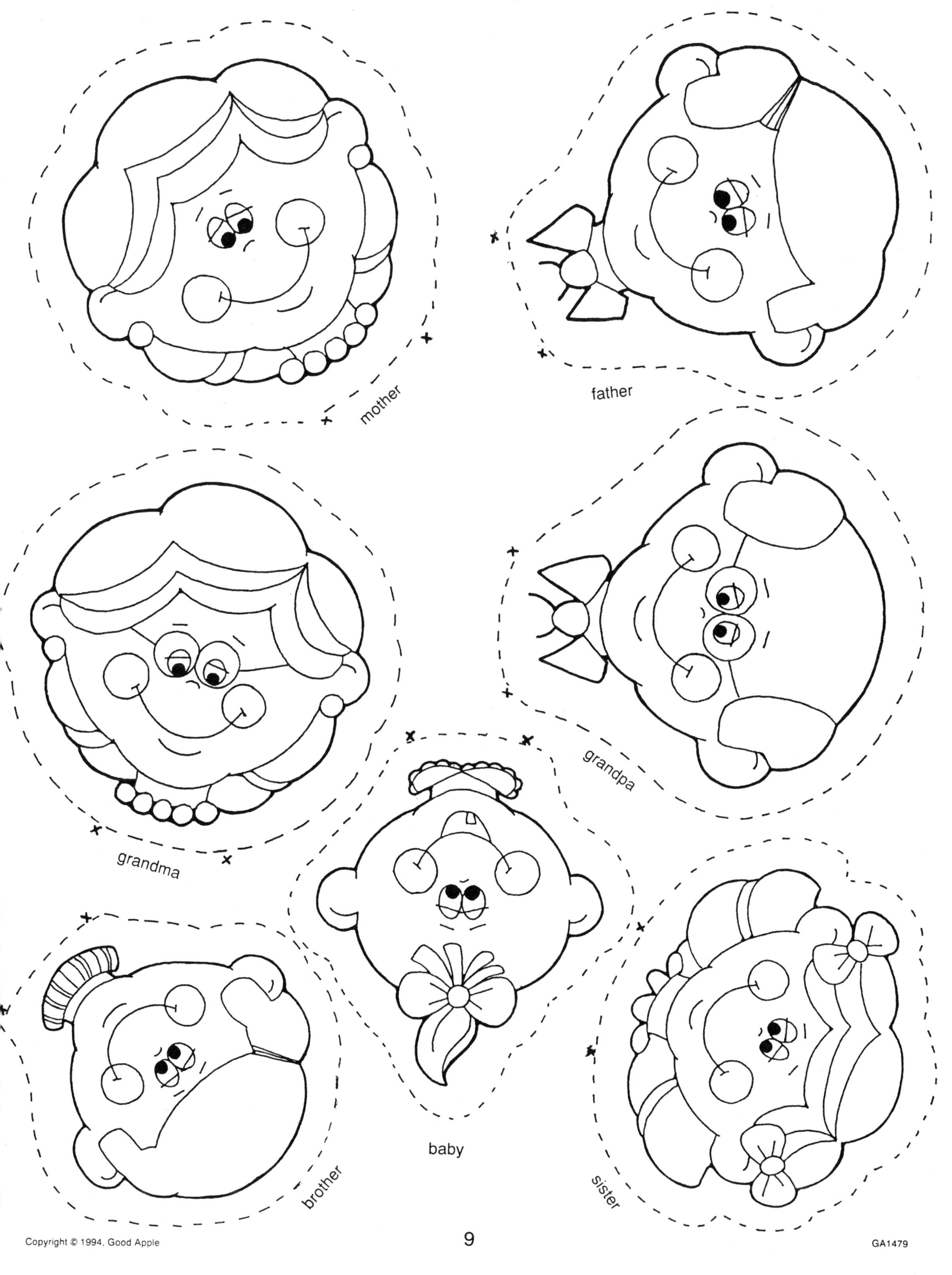
mother
father
grandma
grandpa
baby
brother
sister

tall man
pinky
thumb man
pointer man
goblin
clown
lazy man

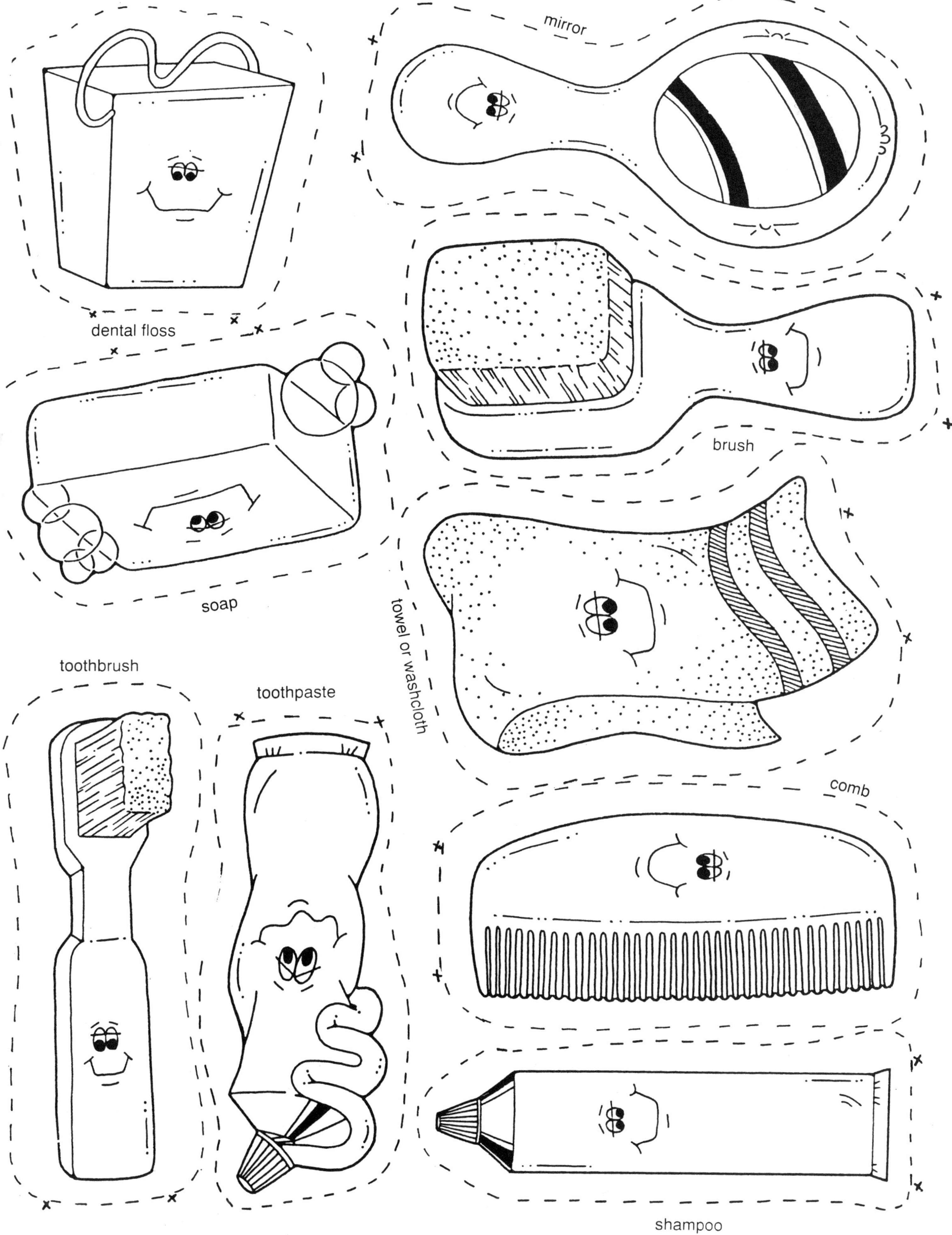
mirror
dental floss
brush
soap
towel or washcloth
toothbrush
toothpaste
comb
shampoo

plane
helicopter
train
car
truck
boat

grapes
pear
orange
watermelon
lemon
cherries
banana
apple
plum

squash
onion
potato
corn
turnip
pepper
tomato
broccoli

MILK
milk
lettuce
carrot
eggs
cheese
radish
bean
bread

sucker
pie
lollipop
CHOCOLATE
candy
cake
ice-cream cone

brontosaurus
Tyrannosaurus rex
parasaurolophus
stegosaurus
triceratops
pteranodon

sea horse
octopus
whale
fish
clam
starfish
shark
snail

freckle-faced bear
happy-faced bear
sad-faced bear
round-faced bear
thin-faced bear
long-chinned bear

bear
lion
deer
elephant
tiger
monkey

horse
pig
cat
lamb
dog
cow

squirrel
rabbit
frog
duck
mouse
beaver
chicken

turtle
butterfly
bird
owl
worm
ladybug
bee
caterpillar

cloud
moon
sun
star
snowflake

tulip
shamrock
flower
kite
raindrop
leprechaun

firecrackers
balloon
baseball
balloon
ball
heart

witch
bat
ghost
monster
spider
jack-o'-lantern

Pilgrim girl
Indian
turkey
Pilgrim boy
acorn
scarecrow

candy cane
Mr. Snowman
Mrs. Snowman
elf
Christmas tree
Mrs. Claus
Santa Claus

octagon
star
triangle

heart
square
rectangle
circle
diamond
oval

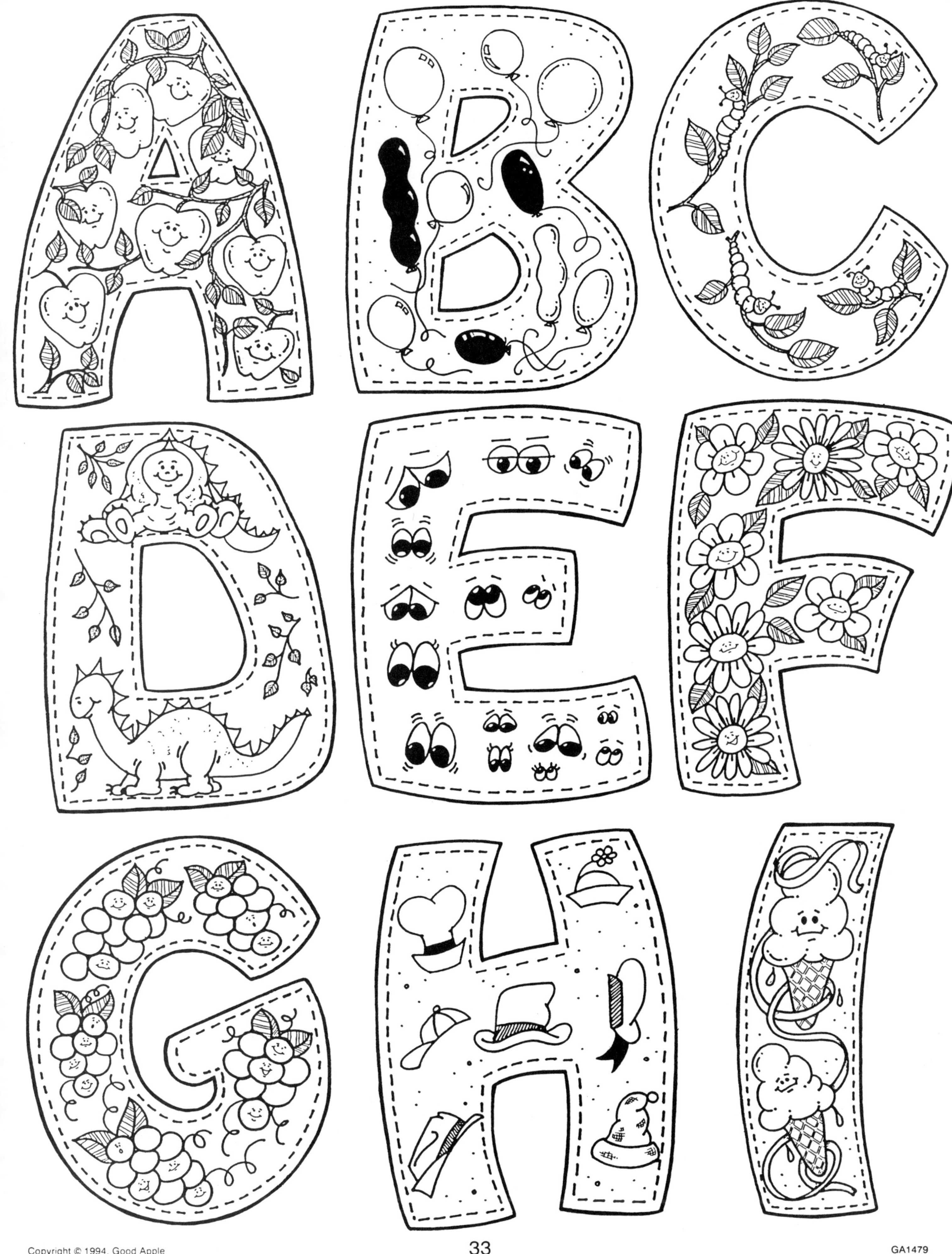

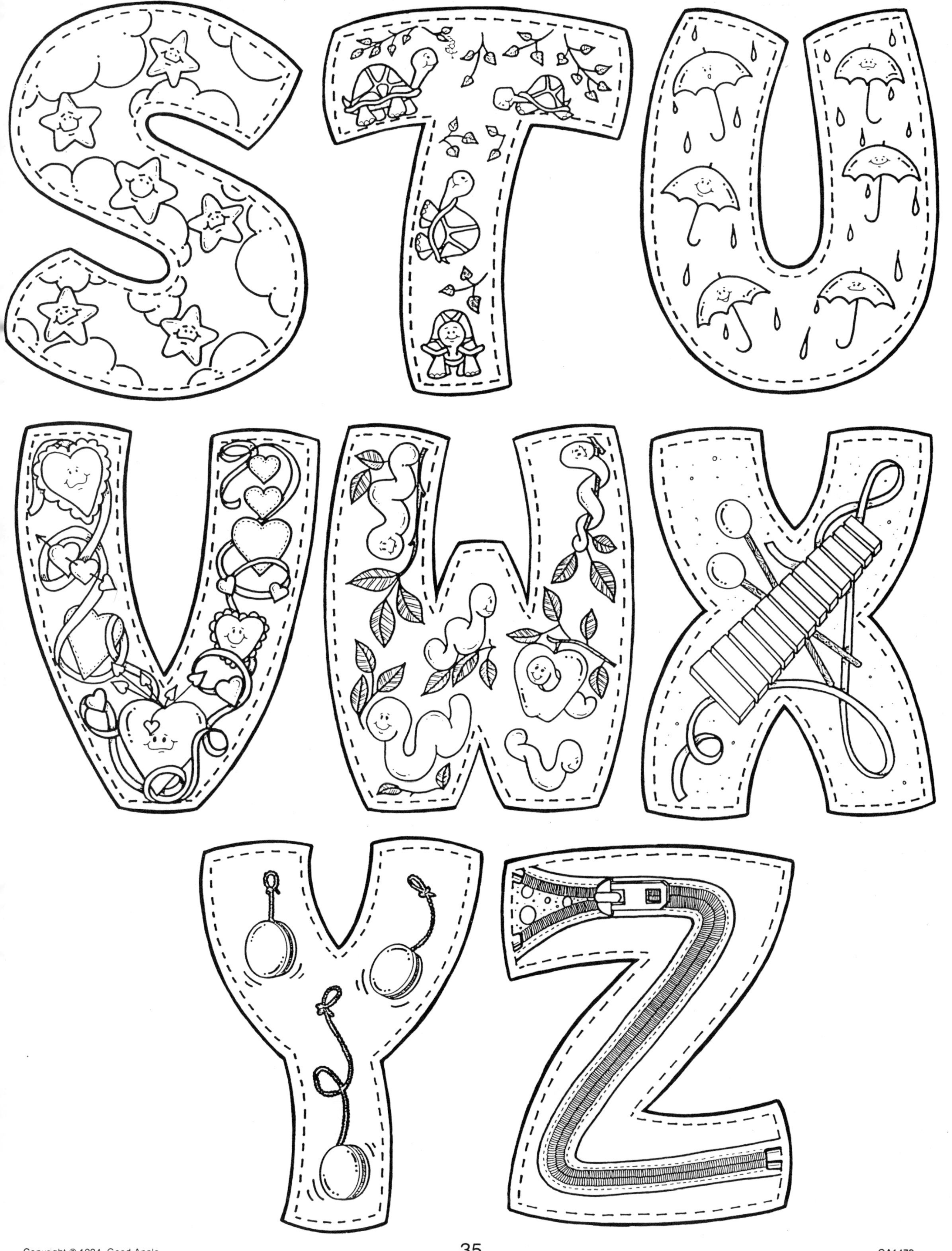

Poems and Verses

Shapes

Throughout the neighborhood are many shapes that we use every day. See if you can find them as you take a walk today. They appear most everywhere you look.

Cyd Circle

is the shape of a ball. She loves to bounce everywhere and play in many games.

Ollie Octagon

is a stop sign shape. He tells people when they should stop and look both ways before crossing the street.

Danny Diamond

is the shape of a baseball field. After he hits the ball, he runs as fast as he can to every corner till he's home again.

Susie Star

is the shape of the star on the top of the Christmas tree. She sparkles and glimmers proudly all the time.

Sammy Square

is the shape of boxes wrapped for birthday presents. Some boxes are big and some are small.

Ottis Oval

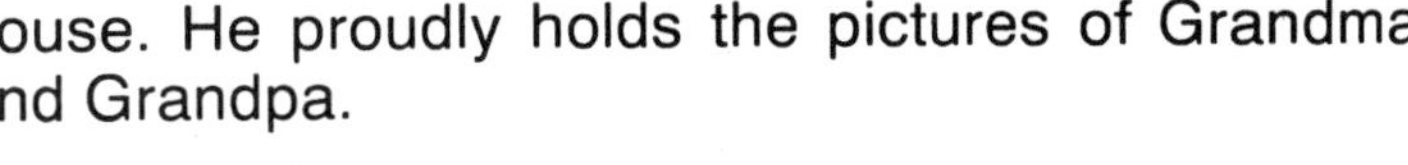

is the shape of picture frames that hang in the house. He proudly holds the pictures of Grandma and Grandpa.

Heidi Heart

is the shape of valentines. She proudly shows off her lace and ribbons when she is given to someone she loves.

Randy Rectangle

is the shape of the little red wagon. He loves to have kids sit in him while he gives them a ride through the neighborhood.

Trixie Triangle

is the shape of the roof on a house. She lets the rain slide down her slopes and fall to the ground.

The Alphabet

A is for the apples,
B is for balloons;
C is for the caterpillars
That crawl from room to room.

D is for the dinosaur,
See the eyes on **E**;
F is for the flowers
That smell so good to me.

G is for the grapevine,
H is for the hats;
I is lots of ice cream,
Let's have some for a snack.

J is for the jack-o'-lanterns,
K, let's fly a kite;
L is for a lollipop
That I can lick or bite.

M has lots of mushrooms,
N, you'll find a nose;
O is for the octopus,
Look how fast he goes!

P is for the juicy pear,
Q, a question mark;
R is for small raindrops,
Hey! I'm pretty smart!

S is the twinkling little stars,
A turtle climbs a **T**;
U is an umbrella
That covers all of me.

V is for the valentine,
W has worms,
X is for the xylophone
I'd like to try to learn.

Y is for a yo-yo,
A zipper on the **Z**;
Now I know my alphabet;
I'm great, don't you agree?

The Difference

It makes no difference in this world
If everyone you're meeting,
Is just a little different
Than what you're used to greeting.

It makes no difference in this world
If every face is round,
Or even if a face has freckles,
Or even upside down.

It makes no difference in this world
If every face is thin
Or even if you have big ears,
Or an extra long, long chin.

It makes no difference in this world
How others look to us,
But what really makes the difference
Is a smile, that's a must.

What really makes the difference here
Is not the way you're shaped,
But the frown that comes across the face
And the ugly way it's draped.

What really makes the difference here
Is the smile that you wear,
For it tells all... and who you are,
And lets others know you care.

(Use the bear puppets on page 19.)

The Circus Clown

I love to watch the circus acts,
Especially the clowns,
They always seem to make me laugh,
With their noses big and round.

A silly face and funny hats,
They always make me smile;
Wouldn't it be lots of fun
To clown around awhile.

Stars

This star can twinkle,
This star can shine,
He loves to sparkle,
I'm glad he's mine.

Snowflakes

One lacy snowflake
Comes fluttering down,
Two little snowflakes
Dancing to the ground.
Three lacy snowflakes
Another makes four.
Four lacy snowflakes
Welcome many more.

Animals

Too bad I'm not an elephant,
My nose would be quite long;
If I were a striped tiger,
A growl would be my song.

The lion is my favorite choice,
My hair would be a mane,
They never have to keep it brushed,
I wish I were the same.

But since I'm just a little kid,
I like the way I am;
But mother says sometimes I act
Just like I'm one of them.

Caterpillars

Fuzzy little caterpillar,
Give him lots of room;
He's very busy in the tree
Building a cocoon.

Fuzzy little caterpillar,
Where are you today?
He's turned into a butterfly;
See him fly away.

Can You Guess What I Am?

I'm sweet and almost yellow
My mess you'll have to bear,
But I'm tasty and delicious;
Can you guess me? I'm a pear.

My skin is kind of bumpy
I'm green most of the time,
I have a sour, puckery taste;
Can you guess me? I'm a lime.

I'm so juicy and delicious
When I'm picked right off the tree,
I'm a red and juicy apple,
I'm as tasty as can be.

I grow in jungle climate
I'm what monkeys love to munch,
They call me a banana,
Just try me in your lunch.

My color is quite pretty;
Don't think that it is glum,
I'm purple and I'm juicy;
Did you guess that I'm a plum?

Mom makes me into jelly
And a juice that tastes real fine,
I'm a tasty little critter,
I'm a grape right off the vine.

I'm not as big as other fruits,
My taste is just as sweet;
I make a mighty tastin' pie
Of cherries, what a treat!

I love to go on picnic trips
My seeds can make a mess,
A watermelon is my name,
You made a clever guess.

My shape is like another fruit
My skin is called a rind;
Don't mistake me, I'm a lemon;
I taste sour like a lime.

Did you guess them all correctly
The fruits we like to eat?
They're better for your body
Than a sack of sugar treats.

Balloons

My balloons are each shaped differently,
Let's count them one, two, three,
They're red and yellow, and this one's blue,
Each pretty as can be.

Foods

Mother taught me something
That every kid should know,
It's about the things I'm eating
And the way they help me grow.

She said I should be careful
About the cakes and pies,
For if I eat more than a piece
I'll double up in size.

She's constantly reminding me
That bread and eggs and cheese,
Are there to help my body
And to help my brain achieve.

At times when I eat ice cream
And candy way too much,
I should have had the milk instead
And left the junk untouched.

She says life can be short or long,
The decision is up to me.
For coffee and cigarettes
Are things that I don't need.

So listen to your mother
For every kid should know,
That everything you're eating
Will determine how you'll grow.

Numbers

The numbers came to my house
They stayed there for the day,
They marched on in and sat right down
And asked if they could play.

ONE, he stood and counted
TWO, he sang some songs
THREE, he did a cartwheel
FOUR, he hid my thongs.

FIVE, he pulled some faces
SIX, he threw a ball
SEVEN didn't catch it
And it rolled down the hall.

EIGHT, he played piano
NINE, he broke a dish
ZERO put his fingers
In the bowl with fish.

As the day grew to an end
The numbers said good-bye,
And then I heard my clock ring out
To wake my sleepy eyes.

Colors

Three very important colors
Are red, yellow and blue,
When they are mixed together
The colors are more than a few.

Red and yellow when stirred around
Make an orange you just can't beat,
Blue and red make a nice color too
Of a purple that's really neat.

Yellow and blue when mixed right up
Make a pretty shade of green,
Now mix up all the colors
And brown comes on the scene.

Black and white are shading tones,
They go from dark to light;
No matter how you mix them up
To you, they are just right.

By adding another color
To the yellow, red or blue,
We get so many colors,
Just see what you can do.

(Use balloon patterns or a variety of different patterns that represent the colors stated.)

Snowman

Let's go build a snowman,
We have some time today;
Grab a carrot for his nose,
A scarf that's striped and frayed.

Let's also build a girl one,
The bonnet's for her head,
We'll pretend they dance around
While we are tucked in bed.

Little Bird

Little bird, little bird
High up in a tree;
Come, sing a happy song,
Sing it just for me.

Baby Sister

by Alisa Bates

I have a baby sister,
She's cute as she can be;
But she is very delicate,
Not rough and tough like me.

Baby sister doesn't play trucks
Or throw footballs around,
She just kicks her legs and wiggles,
She scarcely makes a sound.

But baby screams when she gets hurt,
So I will stay away;
I won't bother baby sister
Until she's big enough to play.

My Trip

If I were to take a trip,
I'd love to take a train,
I'd also love to fly up high
And ride inside a plane.

I'd love to travel in a boat
And see the water blue;
Or ride inside a car or truck,
I'd go see something new.

When it's time to take that trip,
It needn't be too far,
And I can go because we have
Boats, planes, trains, trucks and cars.

I Love Little Pussy

Traditional

I love little pussy,
Her coat is so warm,
And if I don't hurt her,
She'll do me no harm;
I'll sit by the fire
And give her some food,
And pussy will love me
Because I am good.

Old MacDonald Had a Farm

Traditional

Old MacDonald had a farm,
Eeigh, aye, eeigh, aye, oh!
And on this farm he had a cow,
Eeigh, aye, eeigh, aye, oh!
With a moo moo here,
And a moo moo there,
Here a moo, there a moo,
Everywhere a moo moo.
Old MacDonald had a farm
Eeigh, aye, eeigh, aye, oh!

(Continue on with other farm animals.)

Five Little Monkeys

Traditional

Five little monkeys jumping on the bed,
One fell off and broke his head;
Mother called the doctor, the doctor said,
"No more monkeys jumping on the bed."

(Continue on 4-3-2-1)

Five Little Ducks

Traditional

Five little ducks went out to play,
Over the hills and far away.
Mother duck said,
"Quack, quack, quack, quack,"
Four little ducks came waddling back.

(Repeat 3-2-1)

No little ducks came waddling back
From over the hills and far away,
Father duck said,
"Quack, quack, quack, quack,"
All the ducks came waddling back.

Twinkle, Twinkle, Little Star

Traditional

Twinkle, twinkle, little star,
How I wonder what you are;
Up above the world so high,
Like a diamond in the sky,
Twinkle, twinkle, little star,
How I wonder what you are.

The Sea

I wonder if a clam gets tired
All tucked inside his shell.
Not getting out to play all day,
I suppose he wouldn't tell.

I wonder if the turtle likes
To crawl around all day,
Supposing he could crawl right out
Of that shell and run and play.

I wonder if the octopus
Is getting just plain weary
Of dragging all around his legs,
His life seems awfully dreary.

I wonder if the many fish
Would like to walk around
Instead of swishing here and there,
But, I suppose they'd drown.

I wonder if the great big whale
Would ever be content
With living in the mountains
In a cabin or a tent.

I don't suppose they'd want a change,
The critters of the sea,
That's why they're there and I am here
In this big world made for me.

Ice Cream

Take a lick of ice cream,
A cool and scrumptious treat;
There are so many kinds
Of flavors left to eat.

There is one drawback though,
For good as it might taste;
You want to eat too much,
And it goes to your waist.

This Little Pig

English Finger Play

This little pig went to market,
This little pig stayed home;
This little pig had roast beef,
This little pig had none;
This little pig cried, "Wee, wee, wee,"
All the way home.

Eency Weency Spider

English Finger Play

Eency weency spider went up the waterspout,
Down came the rain and washed the spider out.
Out came the sun and dried up all the rain,
Then the eency weency spider went up the spout again.

Where Is Thumbkin?

English Finger Play

Where is Thumbkin? Where is Thumbkin?
Here I am. Here I am.
How are you today, sir?
Very well I thank you,
Run away, run away.
Where is Pointer?
Where is Tall Man?
Where is Lazy Man?
Where is Pinky?
Where are all the men?

Animal Sounds

A frog says "rib-bit,"
A bird says "tweet,"
A turkey says "gobble,"
And a chick says "peep."

A duck says "quack, quack,"
A cow says "moo-oo,"
Little lambs say "baa, baa,"
And an owl says "who-oo."

Imitate their sounds,
It's fun to do,
Let's say it together,
"Rib-bit," "quack," "moo."

My Garden

I planted in my garden
Some very tiny seeds;
I water and care for them,
I pull out all the weeds.

When they've grown and ripened,
My radishes and beans,
I'll serve them up for dinner
With a plate of lettuce greens.

The peppers and tomatoes
The onions and the beets,
Have colors bright and cheery
That are also fun to eat.

Let's not forget the carrots,
The rabbits they will please;
And broccoli is so tasty
With a sauce of creamy cheese.

And in my little garden
I grew a hundred ears,
They're not the kind that's on my head,
It's corn! So hide your fears.

Lots of eyes keep watching me
But I am not surprised;
The eyes are on potatoes,
I like them baked or fried.

The pumpkin is the nicest thing
To always have around;
From spooky jack-o'-lanterns
To the tastiest pie in town.

I'm glad I planted my garden,
For now I get to see
What little seeds grow into;
Such delicious food for me.

My Family

My father is so brave and strong,
My mother, loving and dear,
My brother helps me learn new things,
And I know my sister cares.

My grandma always has a hug,
Grandpa, a story or two;
I know my family loves me a lot
And they know I love them too.

Ladybug Lucy, Butterfly Sue

Ladybug Lucy,
Butterfly Sue,
The sun is here to warm your wings,
The flowers love you too.

Ladybug Lucy,
Butterfly Sue,
It's time to fly back to your homes,
The night is calling you.

Halloween

You never know who's behind the door,
A spider, a monster, witches galore.
It could be a goblin or a black cat,
It could be a ghost or a low-flying bat.
Beware! Don't answer on Halloween night,
Unless you're prepared for a terrible fright!

Teddy Bear

I love little teddy bear
With its little button nose;
Its fur is soft and fuzzy
From its head down to its toes.

Oh fuzzy bear, fuzzy bear,
With your little button nose;
Oh cuddly bear, cuddly bear,
I love to snuggle you close.

Weather

I am happy for the sunshine
That brightens up the day,
And the patter of the raindrops
As they fall their merry way.

I shout for joy at snowflakes
As they cover me with white,
And the lightning doesn't scare me,
But the thunder does a might.

The clouds, they look like cotton,
They're different every day,
I dream they're ships and dragons
And animals at play.

I love to sit and linger,
As the night draws to a still,
And watch the stars and moonshine
Light up the sky they fill.

It's nice to know the good things,
The things that I can see
Are things that give me pleasure,
That I can watch for free.

Acorns

Funny little acorn
Right now you're just a seed,
But later on you'll grow real tall,
And grow into a tree.

The Worm

See him crawling on the ground,
He isn't very fast,
He wiggles as he scoots along,
The worm is here at last.

Dinosaurs! Dinosaurs! Dinosaurs!

Last night I dreamed I was a dinosaur. Not just one dinosaur, but six different dinosaurs! What a busy night I had. First I was a **brontosaurus**. You know which ones they are, don't you? They are the great big ones that eat lots of twigs and leaves. Boy! Did I make a lot of noise when I walked around. Mom thinks I'm noisy when I'm awake; well, she should have heard me last night. Then I turned into a **Tyrannosaurus rex**. I had a great time chasing all the other dinosaurs on my hind legs. But I sure looked funny with those two tiny legs up front. They didn't help me at all, especially when I tripped over a log. My teeth were really sharp too. I'd sure hate to brush them all the time.

Next I was a **pteranodon**. They look sort of weird you know. My body was the size of a turkey but my wings were as long as the street in front of our house. I hung upside down and caught a fish right out of the water. Yuck! Raw fish. Thank goodness that didn't last long because I soon changed into a **triceratops**. I was as big as an elephant, and I had three horns coming out of my head. I had a great time ramming into things, but I think if I did that for real, my head would hurt.

Next I was a **stegosaurus**. I think he was my favorite. I had things poking out of my tail and, best of all, I had spikes at the end of it for protection. I sure could have used that at recess last week. Don't worry; I'm almost finished. The very last dinosaur I became was sort of funny looking. I had a beak that looked a lot like a duck's beak. I guess you could call me a duckbill dinosaur, but my real name was **parasaurolophus**. I didn't fight anyone or stomp around really loud or act very mean. But I sure had fun swimming around in the water.

Well, that was the end of my adventure, except I was awfully glad when I woke up to find me and not a dinosaur in my bed. I imagine Mom and Dad were too. I wonder what I'll dream tonight?

The Little Red Hen

Traditional

One day the Little Red Hen was scratching in the farmyard when she found a grain of wheat. "Who will help me plant the wheat?" she said.

"Not I," said the duck.

"Not I," said the cat.

"Not I," said the pig.

"Very well then," said the Little Red Hen, "I will do it myself." So she planted the grain of wheat.

After some time the wheat grew tall and ripe.

"Who will help me cut the wheat?" asked the Little Red Hen.

"Not I," said the duck.

"Not I," said the cat.

"Not I," said the pig.

"Very well then," said the Little Red Hen, "I will cut it myself." And she did.

"Now," said the Little Red Hen, "Who will help me thresh the wheat?"

"Not I," said the duck.

"Not I," said the cat.

"Not I," said the pig.

"Very well then," said the Little Red Hen, "I will thresh it myself." And she did.

When the wheat was threshed, she said, "Who will help me take the wheat to the mill to have it ground into flour?"

"Not I," said the duck.

"Not I," said the cat.

"Not I," said the pig.

"Very well then, I will do it myself," she said. And she did.

When the wheat was ground into flour, she said, "Who will help me make this flour into bread?"

"Not I," said the duck.

"Not I," said the cat.

"Not I," said the pig.

"Very well then, I will do it myself," said the Little Red Hen, and she baked a lovely loaf of bread.

Then she said, "Who will help me eat the bread?"

"I will," said the duck.

"I will," said the cat.

"I will," said the pig.

"Oh, no you won't!" said the Little Red Hen.
"I will eat it myself." And she did.